HISTORY

OF

THE SOCIETY

FOR

𝕻romoting 𝕮hristian 𝕶nowledge

IN

BENGAL,

FROM 1714 TO 1847.

CALCUTTA : 1846.

SOCIETY FOR PROMOTING CHRISTIAN KNOWLEDGE,

MISSION ROW.

HISTORY

OF THE

Society for Promoting Christian Knowledge

IN

BENGAL.

IN the beginning of last century the tide of public opinion in England ran very strong against any plan for imparting knowledge to the lower classes. By some it was argued, that teaching the poor to read would certainly lead them to be rebels to the government: others contended, that it would render them thoroughly discontented; while a few actually propounded the opinion, that if writing were taught, the crime of forgery would be increased to an enormous extent.

These prejudices still lingered in the breasts of many as late as the commencement of this century, of which we have an instance in the history of Hannah More's establishment of schools at Chedder. But this opposition to popular education was not universal; and to the Society for Promoting Christian Knowledge must be ascribed the high honour of having been the *first* public body in England which supported and advocated the enlightenment of the people. So convinced were the members of the Society of the intimate connexion between vice and spiritual ignorance, that at the very first meeting they held on the formation of their Society in 1698, they agreed to consider " how to further and promote that good design of erecting Catechetical Schools in each parish, in and about London." They soon directed their efforts to the country also; and in 1741 more than 2000 schools had been founded, principally through the instrumentality of the Society. The Anniversary Sermons preached at St. Paul's, also powerfully contributed to keep public attention alive to the question of national education; and in 1839, the Society for Promoting Christian Knowledge granted £5000 to promote the object of the National Society. It also, a century since, propounded the plan, so successfully acted on in modern times in Switzerland by Fellenberg, of having Schools of Industry, so as to combine education with instruction; and thus not merely to improve the intellectual powers, but, also, to form the habits, and accustom the pupils to a life of manual labour.

But its exertions were not limited to England. In 1709 it established parochial libraries in some of the West India islands; and a century ago, contributed liberally to translations and editions of the Scriptures in the Arabic, Gaelic, and Welsh languages. The spiritually destitute colonists of Africa; the deeply debased convicts of Australia; the wild tribes of New Zealand; and the masses of English emigrants to Australia, have engaged the sympathies of the friends of the Society. Aid has also been extended towards augmenting the number of churches and schools in China. It has granted the munificent sum of £10,000 to the Fund for Endowing Colonial Bishoprics. The following is a general view of its operations last year, recently prepared by the Rev. T. B. Murray, one of the Secretaries :—

" The Society for Promoting Christian Knowledge distributes at reduced prices, Bibles, New Testaments, Common Prayer-books, and religious publications, among the Poor; assists in supplying Schools with books of instruction; and aids necessitous parishes in England and Wales with gratuitous grants of books and tracts for National Schools, Lending Libraries, Distribution, &c.

" Great assistance has been rendered by grants of large Bibles and Common Prayer-books for the performance of Divine Service, in new Churches and Chapels erected by means of private contributions, and in School-rooms licensed by the Bishops.

" The Society has long imparted its benefits to Hospitals and Prisons, the Army and Navy, the Coast Guard Service, Tide-Waiters, Bargemen, Fishermen, Emigrants, &c. Measures have recently been taken for encouraging the formation of Lending Libraries, for the use of the Metropolitan and City Police; those bodies being allowed, on the application of the superintendents, to receive books and tracts, from the Permanent Catalogue, at twenty-five per cent. under the cost price.

" The Society has laboured greatly to advance Christianity in the West Indies. Besides smaller grants, it gave £10,000 at one vote, for the religious instruction of the negroes. On the occasion of the dreadful hurricane in August, 1831, which destroyed nearly all the churches and schools in Barbadoes, the Society contributed £2000 towards their restoration. It also granted £1000 towards rebuilding the churches and schools destroyed in Antigua by the earthquake of February, 1843.

" Aid has been extended to Australia, Van Diemen's Land, New Zealand, Upper and Lower Canada, Nova Scotia, Newfoundland, Bermuda, New Brunswick, Prince Edward's Island, the Cape of Good Hope, the Mauritius, Gibraltar, Malta, Asia Minor, Athens, Egypt, Syria, and the Holy Land. Efforts have also been made towards promoting the Society's objects in China. The sum of £2000 has lately been voted towards the erection of a Bishoprick in our Chinese possessions. Besides this, assistance has been given towards the erection of a church at Hong Kong, and for supplies of books.

" The total number of Books and Tracts circulated between April 1845, and April 1846, has amounted to *Four Millions Four Hundred and Fifty-one Thousand Six Hundred and Twenty:* viz. Bibles, 115,941; New Testaments, 89,609; and Prayer-books,

285,044 : other bound Books and Tracts, 665,543; unbound Tracts, 3,295,483.

" The sale of Books and Tracts in the retail department of the Depositories in Great Queen-street, and the Royal Exchange, has amounted during the year to upwards of £13,993.

" From the year 1738, when the Society first began to report its annual issues of publications, to the present year, 1847, it is calculated that it has distributed upwards of *eighty-two millions* of books and tracts."

While at the commencement of last century the Society for Propagating the Gospel devoted its attention to the spiritual welfare of the slaves of the West India isles and of the British settlers in North America, the swarthy inhabitants of Hindustan called forth the sympathies of the Society for Promoting Christian Knowledge; and at a period when it was remarked that " the breast of every Englishman, who went to India, was an altar to Mammon," the same Society showed by its acts, that the flame of Christian philanthropy burned bright in the hearts of many in England. The missionary labours of Schwartz, and his upright acts, which elicited the approbation both of Musalman princes and the East India Company, were sustained by the Society for Promoting Christian Knowledge, who also afforded their aid to Ziegenbalg and his associates.

To those anxious to have a brief account of their labours, we would strongly recommend the perusal of the first number of The Calcutta Review, which gives an able article on " The Earliest Protestant Mission to India." The Society, from its exertions in India, is well entitled to the following eulogium:—" The Society for Promoting Christian Knowledge kept the dying sparks of missionary zeal alive, and prevented its entire extinction, when buried under the general forgetfulness of all the Protestant Churches;" and in " Campbell's British

India," the work of a Dissenting minister, the following testimony is borne to its usefulness:—"As the Society for Promoting Christian Knowledge was the first Society in the field; as it was established in an age when no efforts were made by any other denomination to propagate the Gospel; as it has numbered among its missionaries some of the most devoted and illustrious of men, and has done a great work, which now, while I write, it makes my heart glad and reflects an honour on my country; it is impossible but to speak in terms of commendation and gratitude. May its former spirit, and labours, and success, be revived, and may it yet appear a bright luminary to enlighten the world!" The first printing press that British India saw was established by the Society for Promoting Christian Knowledge, in 1711, at Madras; and in 1714, an edition of the Tamul New Testament issued from it. Through the Society, in modern times, the first dawn of Gospel light broke on Hindustan; and, as the Report of 1824 states, "it is the oldest Society existing: it is a Bible Society, a Church Missionary Society, a School Society, and a School-book Society."

To the Society for Promoting Christian Knowledge belongs the distinguished honour of having sent the *first* Protestant Missionary to Bengal, the Rev. J. Kiernander, in 1758; and of having, previously to that period, fanned the flame of missionary enterprise. We find that, previous to 1709, the Society found a correspondent in the Rev. S. Briercliffe, chaplain of Calcutta —the *only* chaplain in Bengal at that period: he offered to superintend a school in Calcutta, and mentions the openings presented by a number of natives that had been kidnapped by the Portuguese, who carried on the slave trade extensively at that period in Bengal, gaining numerous proselytes by first enslaving the natives in order to baptize them.[a] The Society sent him a packet of books.   In 1709 the Society for Promoting Christian Knowledge sent out a circulating library to Calcutta, the first in India; and in 1731 a Charity School was opened in Calcutta, under its auspices.   The pupils in it were clothed in the same manner as the boys of the Blue Coat School in London, and were taught by Padre Aquiere, formerly a Franciscan friar at Goa.   In 1732, the Rev. G. Bellamy, chaplain, received another supply of books; he was a corresponding member of the Society, and was suffocated in the Black Hole of Calcutta in 1756, when the city was taken by the Musalmans.   In 1732, the Society for Promoting Christian Knowledge offered to contribute to the support of a missionary to Bengal, as a number of Dutchmen and Germans interested themselves in the question, but no suitable person could then be found at Halle, though it subsequently became a second Iona, and was the source for supplying missionaries, when there was little zeal in the Anglican clergy to embark on the errand of mercy.

We now proceed to notice the career of one of the most useful and disinterested missionaries of the Society for Promoting Christian Knowledge, that ever trod the shores of India,—the late Rev. J. Kiernander,—a man who made India his *home* at a period when Europeans were either "birds of prey or birds of passage," and who devoted above £12,000 of his own money to charitable

---

[a] This was the mode by which the class called Portuguese became so numerous in various parts of India; and the evil reached such a height, that in 1751 the English Government at Madras was obliged to issue an order, that for the future no person should cause his slaves to be made proselytes to the Popish faith under penalty of losing them.

objects. And yet, such a man has been branded with infamy by Mr. Carne, in his " Lives of Eminent Missionaries." This is to be attributed to Mr. Carne's want of correct information, and his drawing his data from prejudiced sources. The author of an able paper in the Calcutta Review for March, 1847, points out a number of Mr. Carne's mistakes and inaccuracies.[b]

The Rev. J. Kiernander, the *first* Protestant missionary to Bengal, was born in Sweden, 1711. His uncles were colonels in the army of " the illustrious madman," Charles the Twelfth, and were killed at the battle of Pultowa. Mr. Kiernander studied at the University of Upsal, and from thence proceeded to Halle, then a nursery for missions, and distinguished for its Orphan House, superintended by the indefatigable Franke. Mr. Kiernander studied four years

[b] I have myself examined all the documents in the archives of the Society for Promoting Christian Knowledge, as well as those in Bengal, and fully concur in the observations of the reviewer on Carne's Life of Kiernander. " Mr. Carne's memoir is quite unworthy of the credit it has received, and the conclusions to which it leads are quite unwarranted by real facts. It is a strange mixture of fact and fiction, full of mistakes, which might easily have been corrected by reference to books of history, and to Missionary Reports. It has run together years widely separated in the course of time, mixed up dates and facts having no connexion, given a high colouring to sober statements, and exaggerated not only the good but also the evil. Many things appear in the Memoir, which excite a smile, not to say that they utterly destroy its credit. Mr. Carne's narrative occupies twenty pages, and in this short space there are no less than *forty-five errors of fact*, which might easily have been corrected." His statements respecting Kiernander's life are much akin to his remarks respecting Kiernander's visiting " *mountain* villages " near Calcutta; of " the lofty and precipitous banks of the Hugly;" and of " the deep and lone ravines " of Chandernegore,—though it is a well-known fact that there is not a hill within two hundred miles of Calcutta!

there, and was subsequently appointed superintendent over 2500 orphans. As he was on the eve of returning to Sweden, Franke proposed to him, in the name of the Society for Promoting Christian Knowledge, to go out as a missionary to Cuddalore, near Madras. He accepted the offer, and, like Xavier, returned not to bid farewell to his relations, but proceeded forthwith to London, where he was received most hospitably by the Royal Chaplain, who entertained in his own house all the missionaries who visited London. At that period even royalty did not despise missions, and George the First of England entered into *direct personal correspondence* with the missionaries. He arrived at Madras in 1740—a singular period in Indian history, the English then possessing only a small tract of land of about five square miles at each of their settlements of Bombay, Madras, and Calcutta. France and England were contending for the supremacy in India, and on all sides the din of war was heard; but " Jerusalem was built in troublous times," and Mr. Kiernander prosecuted his labours at Cuddalore in schools, and among natives and Portuguese : though many Europeans, alarmed for their safety, quitted the town, yet he remained behind, and the governor granted him the use of a church, from which he had expelled the Jesuits, on account of their political intrigues with the French. In 1750 he had the pleasure of welcoming Schwartz in the land of his future evangelistic triumphs. But in 1758, Count Lally, the commander of the French troops, breathing out destruction against the Anglo-Indian settlements, and anxious to wreak his vengeance for the wrongs which he considered England had inflicted on his native country, Ireland, attacked Cuddalore, which surrendered to him; but on that occasion he behaved most honourably to Mr. Kiernander, to whom, on applying for protection for the missionaries, he replied,—" That they, as preachers of peace and concord, had nothing to fear from his army, and that he would give strict orders that none of them should be injured, and that their houses should be preserved." He kept his promise to the missionaries, though the property of the English was confiscated, and Kiernander was enabled to quit Cuddalore in time to escape the fangs of the Jesuits, who were very indignant at Lally's showing such kindness to him.

Mr. Kiernander arrived at Calcutta in 1758, having been invited to engage in missions there by the victor of Plassey, Colonel Clive, who had seen the beneficial effects of Mr. Kiernander's labours in the Madras Presidency. He gave him the use of a dwelling-house, and, along with Mr. Watts, a member of council, stood sponsor for his son. Calcutta then presented a widely different aspect from what it does now. No such class as " Young Bengal " at that period existed.

We shall take a short review of the state of Calcutta when Mr. Kiernander arrived in it; it was pre-eminently then " the living solitude of a city of idolaters."—The Sati fires were to be seen frequently blazing, while many widows mounted the pyre with the most perfect resignation, assured by the Brahmins that they should be happy in heaven for as many years as their husbands had hairs on their bodies, which were liberally calculated at the number of thirty-five millions.—Fakirs ranged *ad libitum* through the town in a state of complete nudity, with their clotted hair dangling down to the length of two or three feet, and their bodies besmeared with cow-dung, " the most sacred of Indian cosmetics."— A Hindu, after visiting a European, would have his garments washed to free them from the impurity contracted from a mlechha.— The English language was little known, and Europeans resorted chiefly to signs and gesticulations to communicate with the natives.—A proposal to teach a woman to read would have been regarded in the same light as if it had been suggested in London to instruct monkeys in Hullah's system of singing.

Mr. Kiernander's mission plans were cordially approved of by the two chaplains of Calcutta, who also aided him in raising subscriptions. From the good he saw result from it at the Orphan House of Halle, and from his views of the condition of the Hindus, he gave the preference to catechising, as a means of usefulness, convinced "that by a conscientious discharge of the duty of catechising, he lays the foundation of a fabric that will be only rising into greatness when he (the catechiser) is hastening to decay." He commenced a school in December, 1758, which in a year contained 174 pupils, Brahmans, Portuguese, Armenians, and English; forty-eight of them were educated at the expense of the Society for Promoting Christian Knowledge. He soon beheld some fruit from his labours in the conversion of a Brahman, which was then as great an innovation on the long-cherished prejudices of the Hindus, as the conversion of a cardinal to the Protestant faith would have been in the days of Luther.

Though Mr. Kiernander never acquired the Bengali language, having been so engaged with schools and pastoral duties among the Europeans as to afford him no time or opportunity, yet he laboured very earnestly among the Portuguese, and in 1759, he commenced a service in the Portuguese language, a *patois* very different from the classical tongue of the Lusiad, though it has survived as the last remnant of Lusitanian greatness in India. The power of the Portuguese has vanished like the scenes of a drama; but its language still lingers in India, a memento of the past. Mr. Kiernander employed it as the medium for imparting a higher style of education: it was then used very commonly as the vehicle for communication between Europeans and natives. But British supremacy has long since undermined the influence both of the Portuguese and their language: the English language seems destined now to exercise in India all the sway which the Latin did in former times over the languages and literature of Europe.[c]

In 1762, Calcutta was scourged with an epidemic, which carried off numbers of Europeans; the parents withdrew for a time their children from the school; Mr. Kiernander, however, continued at his post, and his school filled again. Many of his scholars became writers in public offices, and occupied respectable situations in life; thus the seeds of truth sown in the school were extensively scattered. In 1766 he had the pleasure of admitting a Jew into the Christian Church: he was a native of Smyrna. Subsequent efforts have been made among the Jews in Calcutta, but with little success. In 1768, Padri Bento, who had been a Romish missionary in Bengal for fifteen years, became a Protestant, and proved of great service to Mr. Kiernander. He translated part of the Prayer Book into Bengali. Mr. Kiernander was eminently successful in his labours among Romanists, aided by Padri Bento, who was a man of ability, well acquainted with Urdu, Bengali, and Portuguese, so that he became very useful to Mr. Kiernander. In 1769, De Costa, another Popish priest, joined the mission. This spread alarm to Goa itself, and an emissary was sent from thence to convey the converts from Calcutta to Goa, and lodge them in the dungeons of the Inquisition. The plot, however, failed. In 1769 he baptized a Chinese from Canton, the *first* Chinese that was baptized by a Protestant missionary.

[c] There is a very interesting paper on the future influence of the English language in " Douglas on the Advancement of Society."

We now come to an important period in Mr. Kiernander's life, when he had the privilege of erecting a Church in Calcutta,—the Mission Church,—and which has ever since given an impulse to the work of evangelisation under the ministry of Browne, Thomason, &c. Mr. Vansittart, who was Governor of Bengal, and father of Lord Bexley, having required for the use of government the mission house which he had lent to Mr. Kiernander, Mr. Kiernander resolved to build a Church, as Calcutta was then without any sacred edifice for public worship. The building was opened for worship in 1770, and remains to the present day a noble monument of the munificence of its founder. It cost 67,320 rupis, of which only 1818 rupis were raised by subscription; the remainder, 65,502 rupis, was contributed by Mr. Kiernander from his own personal property, as he obtained a large fortune with his wife : and yet, against such a man, who spent £12,000 of his own money in charitable objects, Mr. Carne brings the charge of worldliness, &c. &c.!

This Church, named the Mission Church, was opened in 1770, and continued until 1784, to be the *only* church in Bengal.[d] Service was held in it for two distinct classes of persons—the English residents in Calcutta, and the Portuguese, who required instruction in Christianity

---

[d] At a period when horse-racing on a Sunday was fashionable in Calcutta, — when the only way by which many Europeans there knew the Sabbath, was in seeing the flag-staff hoisted on Fort William, — when many ladies alleged as an excuse for non-attendance at church, that they had no gentlemen to escort them,— Mr. Kiernander presented a bright example of the opposite kind ; he allowed no natives to work at building the Church on Sunday. Lord Hardinge, the late Governor-General, has issued a proclamation, prohibiting persons in government employ from engaging in the public works on Sunday.

almost as much as the heathen. Mr. Kiernander officiated both in English and Portuguese, and devoted his week-days to teaching in the school. We find that in 1771, Mr. Kiernander had ninety-six English communicants, and 104 Portuguese and natives, besides ninety-four pupils in the school. In 1773, Mr. Kiernander's wife died. She bequeathed her jewels to build a school-room; they realised six thousand rupis: and school-rooms were erected on the site of the present Mission Church Rooms. These rooms have been the scene of many missionary meetings held under the superintendence of the Rev. Messrs. Browne, Buchanan, and Thomason.

The Society for Promoting Christian Knowledge, in 1775, sent to Mr. Kiernander a colleague, Mr. Diemer, who had been educated at Halle; he proved a useful labourer, but after eight years' residence he was obliged to return to Europe, in consequence of ill health, the sanitary condition of Calcutta then having been very different from what it is now. The East India Company granted him a free passage to India. They were liberal also on other occasions, as they allowed the Society for Promoting Christian Knowledge, during the last century, to send stationery and other articles, free of freight, to the missionaries in India. The year 1775 was distinguished for the baptism by Mr. Kiernander of Gonesh Das, a well-educated native of Dilhi, who held the important post of Persian translator to the Supreme Court. He was the *first* native who had crossed "the black waters," and bursting through the trammels of caste and the anti-social laws of Hinduism, had visited the shores of England, where he received favourable impressions of Christianity; and on his return, after attending the Mission Church some time, was admitted a member of the Christian Church, and received the name of Robert, after his sponsor, Sir Robert Chambers, who stood forward as an advocate for spreading Christianity among the Hindus, at a period when opinions of the following description were warmly advocated by Anglo-Indians:— " The Hindu system little needs the meliorating hand of the Christian dispensation, for the law is good, if a man use it lawfully."—" No Hindu of respectability will ever yield to the missionary's remonstrances." Even as late as 1808, Major Scott Waring, a Bengal officer, has recorded his opinion in the following terms:—" Whenever the Christian religion does as much for the lower orders of society in Europe, as that of Brahma appears to have done for the Hindus, I shall cheerfully vote for its establishment in Hindustan." [e]

---

[e] We give the following as specimens of the notions and practices of some of the Anglo-Indians in Bengal, in former days, and which proved mighty obstacles to the conversion of the heathen. Colonel Stewart, who received the *sobriquet* of Hindu Stewart, resided at Berhampur, where he worshipped idols and the Ganges; he built a temple at Sagar; and, on his return to Europe, took idols with him to perform puja. Warren Hastings sent an embassy to the Grand Lama to congratulate him on his *incarnation.* Mr. Lushington, a Director of the East India Company, stated publicly, in 1793, " that were 100,000 natives converted, he should hold it as the greatest calamity that could befal India." The sermon preached at Bishop Middleton's consecration, in 1814, was not published, lest the fears of many Anglo-Indians should be excited. At that period, the opponents of missions declared, that if bishops were sent to India, " our empire there would not be worth a year's purchase." Major Scott Waring writes in 1805:—" I never met with a happier race of men than the Hindus, when left to the undisturbed performance of the rites of their own religion; and it might truly be said, that if Arcadian happiness ever had existence, it must have been rivalled in Hindustan." In 1793, a member of the Court of Proprietors declared at the India House, " that the sending missionaries into our Eastern territories is the most wild, extravagant, expensive, unjustifiable project that was ever suggested by the most

During several years previous to 1781, Mr. Kiernander lost his sight; his son, however, who was a layman, read prayers and a sermon in the Church: this practice is observed at the present day in various stations in India and the Colonies, where there is no clergyman. In Calcutta, at the commencement of last century, there was no chaplain in the city, and the service was read by a merchant, who was allowed £50 per annum for his services. The first Governor of Calcutta, Job Charnock, cared so little for religion, that it was said, the only sign of any regard for Christianity he ever exhibited was, that when his *Hindu* wife died, instead of burning he *buried* her. But an unexpected event, in 1787, was about to put a sudden termination to Mr. Kiernander's connexion with the Mission Church; he had affixed his name as security to a bond in favour of his son; the son was unable to pay; the creditors in consequence laid an attachment on Mr. Kiernander's property, and the Mission Church was put up for sale by the sheriff. In this emergency, however, Mr. C. Grant, a warm friend to India, stepped forward and redeemed it for ten thousand rupis. He made it over to the Society for Promoting Christian Knowledge for the use of the mission, and invested the property in the hands of three trustees— Mr. W. Chambers, the Rev. D. Browne, and Mr. Grant himself. An urgent appeal was made to the Society for Promoting Christian Knowledge to send out missionaries; but the Church at that period was sunk in the selfish-

visionary speculator: that the project would affect the ultimate security of our Eastern possessions." We need not be surprised, however, at these statements, when we find the Bishop of St. Asaph stating in the House of Lords, in 1783, that "the obligation said to be incumbent on Christians, to promote their faith throughout the world, had ceased with the supernatural gifts which attended the commission of the Apostles."

ness of mere home exertions, and *no one* volunteered, except the Rev. T. Clarke, of Cambridge, who left England for the Mission Church in 1789. He was welcomed by Lord Cornwallis, and commenced the study of Persian; but in 1790, without giving any previous notice, he dissolved his connexion with the Society for Promoting Christian Knowledge, and accepted a chaplaincy. The Mission Church would have been closed had not the Rev. D. Browne come forward and offered his services, without fee or reward, which he continued till the close of his life. A similar complaint of the aversion of English clergymen to go out to India as missionaries is still to be made. On this subject we extract the following energetic appeal, from a Charge delivered by the Bishop of Calcutta, in 1835 :—

" Oh, that a vision, not of a single man of Macedonia, but of the 134,000,000 of Hindus and Mahometans who are under British sway, or British influence, might present itself to the pious students at our Universities, crying, ' Come over to India and help us.'

" Englishmen, you profess to long for the opportunity of spreading the Gospel, and will you, when the opening is presented, shrink back? Shall men call themselves Christians, and see the scholar, the philosopher, the mere traveller spring forth upon the distant expedition, and not imitate their example for a much higher object?

" Shall Commerce be never weary, never disconcerted in her enterprises; and shall Christianity go to sleep? Shall the Civil and Military Services of India be sought for with avidity by the first families in the kingdom, and shall the service of Christ be declined?

" Shall the privations of a voyage, the languor of an enervating climate, or the increased hazard of disease, never deter men for a moment in every other profession, and shall they deter them in this?

" What can exceed the inviting prospects which India presents ! The fields white for the harvest and awaiting the hand of the reaper! Nations bursting the intellectual sleep of thirty centuries! Superstitions no longer in the giant strength of youth, but doting to their fall. Britain placed at the head of the most extensive empire ever consigned to a Western sceptre—that is, the only great power of Europe professing the Protestant faith, entrusted with the thronging nations of Asia, whom she alone could teach. A paternal government, employing every year of tranquillity in elevating and blessing the people unexpectedly thrown upon its protection.

" No devastating plague as in Egypt — no intestine wars — no despotic heathen or Mahommedan dominion prowling for its prey. But legislation going forth with her laws; science lighting her lamp; education scattering the seeds of knowledge; commerce widening her means of intercourse; the British power ever ready to throw her ægis around the pious and discreet missionary.

" Oh, where are the first propagators and professors of Christianity? Where are our Martyrs and Reformers? Where are the ingenuous, devoted, pious sons of our Universities? Where are our younger devoted clergy? Are they studying their ease? Are they resolved on a ministry tame, ordinary, agreeable to the flesh? Are they drivelling after minute literature, poetry, fame? Do they shrink from that toil and labour, which, as Augustine says, OUR COMMANDER, Noster Imperator, accounts most blessed?[f]

" No: the truth is, honoured brethren, our English youth and English clergymen are uninformed, unread in Eastern story. A death-like obscurity hangs over so distant a scene. They know little of the fortunes of the Indian Church. They think of nothing but persecutions, exile, disease, and death, as connected with the missionary life. They are held back by *a false humility*. They are retained by the tears of sisters and friends. Let us unite, then, in removing misconceptions — let us join in appealing to societies — let us write to particular friends and public bodies — let us afford correct, intelligible information. Let us send specific and individual invitations — and let us pray the

---

[f] " Nihil est in hac vita facilius, maxime hoc tempore, et lætius, et hominibus acceptabilius, Episcopi aut Presbyteri officio, si perfunctorie atque adulatorie res agatur. Nihil est in vita, et maxime hoc tempore difficilius, laboriosius, et periculosius Episcopi vel Presbyteri officio, sed apud Deum nihil beatius, si eo modo militetur quo *noster Imperator* jubet."

' Lord of the harvest, that he would send forth more labourers into his harvest.'

"A false notion prevails that it is a sort of martyrdom to come out to India as a Missionary. Whereas the real danger is on the side of ease, not privation. A young man in the military service has vastly more to encounter. A Missionary in India has more than the comforts of a good English Curacy. THE SINGLE REAL DIFFICULTY IS AN INCREASED HAZARD OF DISEASE. Fifty clergymen are now wanted for India. In the Southern Missions of the Incorporated Society alone, twelve are indispensable."

Notwithstanding Mr. Clarke's defection, however, the congregation was superintended by the Rev. D. Browne; and, as late as 1804, a few members remained; but soon after that the native congregation became extinct, and a considerable interval elapsed before any further efforts were made by the Anglican Church for missions in Bengal. However, the Church which Mr. Kiernander built has ever since proved a nucleus for efforts in educating and Christianising the natives.

Mr. Kiernander closed his career in peace at Calcutta, in 1799, in the eighty-eighth year of his age, and the forty-first of his residence in Bengal. He never revisited Europe; he was not afflicted with "home sickness." Even in 1762, when Calcutta was scourged with an epidemic, and native parents withdrew their children from the school, he remained at his post; and though his health was in a feeble state, he preferred remaining in Calcutta to returning to Europe, and thereby leave his church destitute of missionary superintendence. Among his converts he reckoned Malays, Macasserese, Chinese, Brahmans, and Jews. He was very active in distributing Bibles and Tracts, and he sent a supply of Arabic Testaments to the Court of the Great Mogul. His generosity was only limited by his means. He spent above £12,000 of his own money in charity. He was held in high estimation by the Society for Promoting Christian Knowledge, who, in 1770, passed a vote of thanks to him "for the distinguished zeal he had shown, and the vast expense he had put himself to in building the Church, and for his constant and unwearied attention to the welfare of the mission."

During the period between the death of Mr. Kiernander in 1799, and the year 1825, the attention of the Society for Promoting Christian Knowledge was directed very little towards Bengal, though in 1813 it petitioned Parliament in favour of throwing open India to evangelistic efforts, and granted Bishop Middleton £1000 to distribute in Bengal.[g]

---

[g] Among the individuals who took a prominent part at that time, the name of C. Grant, father to Lord Glenelg, stands conspicuous. His memory will ever be hallowed as one of the benefactors of India. He proceeded to Bengal in 1767, in a very humble capacity; but raised himself by his industry and integrity to a high post under the government: he became Commercial Resident at Malda, and "in his house the voice of prayer and praise was heard, when all was spiritual death around." He retired from India in 1790; but did not, like many other Europeans, forget the land which gave him wealth and influence. In 1792 he published a valuable pamphlet, "Observations on the State of Society among the Asiatic Subjects of Great Britain." In 1794 he was elected a Director of the East India Company, where he always advocated the policy, that our empire should be founded rather on character than on force, and particularly on our moral and intellectual superiority. He regarded the consideration of the affairs of India as his peculiar province, and as affording sufficient occupation to his mind. In the House of Commons he stood forth with Wilberforce, Thornton, and Babington, in the rank of Christian statesmen. In the Court of Directors he was very anxious to send out good men as chaplains to Bengal; and he was ever forward to rebut the calumnies uttered against missions; hence, in 1807, when a motion was made in the Court of

The Calcutta Diocesan Committee of the Society for
Promoting Christian Knowledge, "the first-fruits of
the Indian Episcopate," was established by a warm
friend to Hindu enlightenment, Bishop Middleton,[h]
in 1815, and was speedily followed by similar com-
mittees in Madras and Bombay; several leading
laymen of Calcutta co-operated with it, as Messrs.
Sherer, Trant, Plowden, Harrington, Bayley, Metcalf:
the Rev. D. Corrie also was a warm friend, and, as
long as he was in Calcutta, invariably attended its
meetings. It soon entered on an active career of
usefulness in distributing Bibles, tracts, prayer books,
school books, in hospitals, prisons, schools, and
among that abandoned class, European sailors. Its
founder, Bishop Middleton, warmly advocated the view
that "as true religion was the best support of government, the inculcation of Christian principle on the
natives would be the only safe and certain measure of
securing to Britons their oriental position." The society

Directors, to recal Dr. Buchanan from Bengal, he defended his
conduct in a speech of two hours' length: he exerted himself also
on a similar occasion in 1814, when the Court of Directors were
about to pass a resolution, censuring their civil and military
servants who encouraged missions.

[h] He repeatedly and earnestly pressed on the Society "that little
progress can be expected in their great work of propagating the
Gospel, unless the mind be *prepared* for the reception of Christianity by some previous instruction." Hence he took, as Le Bas's
Life of Middleton shows, a very warm interest in the spread of
English education among the natives; though when he subscribed
to the Hindu College, the managers were so alarmed, lest the
name of a bishop appearing among the subscribers should deter
the parents from sending their children to the institution, that
they returned the money; and yet some of the alumni of that
college have since become converts to Christianity, and adorn the
Christian life.

showed its sense of the importance of Christian education for Bengal by entering on the sphere of vernacular
schools; for, at a meeting held in 1818, it was resolved
to establish the schools in circles, each of which should
contain four vernacular schools, having an English school
in the centre. We shall now give a brief notice of its
labours in the department of schools, lending libraries,
and translations.

In 1818 the Calcutta Diocesan Committee of the
Society for Promoting Christian Knowledge resolved to
establish native schools in the neighbourhood of Calcutta. The bishop gave 2500 rupis towards them, from
a fund placed at his disposal: donations soon amounted
to 13,000 rupis, and subscriptions to 4200 rupis: the
Governor-General granted 1000 rupis. One school
was erected on a piece of ground given by a *native*
for that purpose; the government presented a piece of
land for another school, and, at the recommendation of
the bishop, " a select class of Bengali scholars at the
Free School was put in training as teachers." It is a
subject of deep regret that this excellent plan has never
been carried out at the Free School, though the governors
cordially approved of it, and even agreed to allow the
boys detained beyond fifteen years, ten rupis a month.

The first school was commenced at Russapugla, a
village where the sons and descendants of Tipu Sultan
are kept as state prisoners; Kasinath Babu gave to the
Society for Promoting Christian Knowledge ten bigahs of
land, and the school soon numbered eighty pupils.
Government also granted for a school a piece of ground
near the Lunatic Hospital of Bhawanipur. In order
to stimulate the teachers, the mode of payment adopted
was to give each teacher six rupis monthly for fifty
boys, with an addition of one rupi for every ten above
that number, until the number of one hundred boys

in each school is completed; this system of paying teachers according to the number and proficiency of their boys is quite in accordance with native usage, and has been attended with great success in many schools.

The schools rose rapidly in efficiency and numbers; at first the children showed a great desire for pecuniary rewards, as at that period they thought they were conferring a *favour* on Europeans by attending; they also were very anxious to devote almost the whole of their time to the study of arithmetic: but instead of the trash taught in the common vernacular schools, such works as the *Niti Katha,* a collection of fables on the plan of Æsop, *Bhugol Britanta,* a geography, and the *History of Joseph,* were introduced.

In the vernacular schools, where all Christian instruction is excluded, we may form a notion of what is inculcated on the minds of the pupils from the opinions propounded in the Hindu sacred books on the following points of natural philosophy.—*Serpents* are said to have proceeded from the tears of Brahma, shed on his being vexed at not producing a second creation by his penances. The world is 3,000,000,000 of miles in extent. *Diamonds* are produced from the sun's rays. The *sun* forms the right eye of Siva, one of the gods, and the *moon* his left. *Dews* come from the moon. *Serpents* are said to hear through their eyes, and to have their feet under their skin. *Mountains,* in former days, had wings and flew about, but the wings were clipped in consequence of mountains sometimes perching on cities, and destroying them!

As to the *morality* taught—one of the works read in all the schools are the poems of Chanak, which are ethical. The following are specimens of the morals inculcated,— " Fresh meat, soft rice newly prepared, living with young women, fresh clarified butter, warm milk and tepid water, are the six things which are beneficial to life." Again, "A wife is requisite for the purpose of having a son, a son is requisite for the purpose of offering funeral cakes, a friend is requisite for assistance in time of need, but wealth is requisite for all purposes." "Possessing plenty of eatables, a good appetite, a handsome wife, a liberal heart, and property, are the sure indications of the meritorious actions of man in his former life."

In 1821, the Marchioness of Hastings, who, like her husband, took a lively interest in native improvement, transferred to the Society for Promoting Christian Knowledge the superintendence of a school which she had established at Barrakpur, and left a sum of money when she was quitting India for its support. In 1821 a school was founded by Bishop Middleton in connexion with St. James's Church, on the model of the English parochial schools. The government gave the ground, and the Society for Promoting Christian Knowledge made a donation of 2000 rupis to it. The school still receives aid from the Society for Promoting Christian Knowledge, and contains now about sixty boys, and forty girls. In 1822 the Society for Promoting Christian Knowledge in England voted £5000 for the promotion of native education in India, and an appeal was made to the public on the subject, which realised considerable contributions. The following are extracts from it:—

" The immense importance of establishing schools for the diffusion, in the first place, of European, and ultimately of Christian knowledge, amongst native children in India, must be admitted by all who have seriously reflected upon the means of propagating the Gospel in the East.

" Little progress can be expected in this great work, unless the mind has been prepared for the reception of Christianity by some previous instruction. This point was repeatedly and earnestly pressed upon the attention of the Society for Promoting Christian

Knowledge, by the late lamented Bishop Middleton. The advantages to be derived from hence appear to be no less highly estimated by Bishop Heber—and the opinion of persons best acquainted with the East accords with the sentiments of these distinguished individuals.

" To make provision for such instruction has long been an object of the Society for Promoting Christian Knowledge ; and it has for a considerable time had Schools for that purpose, under the superintendence and direction of its agents. The success which has attended these exertions, particularly at Calcutta, has answered its warmest expectations. The schools are found to form a bond of union between the European clergy and natives, introducing the missionary to the people in the united character of teacher and benefactor. At the same time he himself thus becomes speedily and accurately acquainted with the language, manners, and opinions of the population at large ; while, by the communication of European knowledge, the foundation upon which the superstition of the heathen rests is gradually and imperceptibly undermined."

The Report of 1822 states, respecting the success that has attended the establishment of the schools :—

" Nor is it a small triumph for the Society to be enabled to say that the *morality* of the Gospel is now, at length, regularly inculcated in the minds of the scholars, who read, with the permission and concurrence of their parents and religious guides, as their daily task, selections from the New Testament, translated into their own tongue. The full benefit of such a system of instruction can hardly be appreciated in the course of a single generation ; but in the children who frequent these schools a moral and intellectual improvement is already discernible,—the regularity of their attendance,—their readiness in acquiring knowledge, their hand-writing, and the accuracy with which they are enabled to answer arithmetical and other questions, exhibit a proficiency such as few parochial schools in England have, in a similar space of time, exceeded."

In 1824, the Society had schools under the superintendence of the missionaries of the Society for the Propagation of the Gospel in Foreign Parts at Haura, containing 450 boys, while at the village of Bali, inhabited by most bigoted Brahmans, there were 100 pupils studying the truths of Scripture. In Kasipur, near Calcutta, there was a circle of schools formed in 1821, and at Baripur one was also maintained, which formed the nucleus of subsequent missionary exertions.

The Report of 1825 states respecting these schools :—

"These seminaries of useful knowledge and virtue are efficiently maintained, and duly supplied with native teachers and books; are, besides, regularly superintended by their respective missionary clergymen from Bishop's College. And though the benefits which the children must derive from the course of instruction which they are now receiving do not immediately appear, yet we trust and believe that much solid good has been effected; and that, as the foundation on which the superstructure of the goodliest temple is afterwards raised, is not visible, except on close inspection, so principles are now inculcated in this first generation, as it were, from which we may hope to behold a moral, and even religious, second and third generation to arise. And here your committee cannot but observe with heartfelt joy, how seldom is *caste*, that was once considered to present so formidable and almost insurmountable a barrier to the instruction of Indian children in the doctrines of Christianity, now urged by their parents as an excuse to keep them from the Society's schools; it has disappeared in an accelerated ratio, like a vapour before the sun."

In 1826, the superintendence of these schools was transferred to the missionaries of the Society for Propagating the Gospel; though the expenses were still defrayed by the Society for Promoting Christian Knowledge, which resolved, however, to confine its attention in India to printing works in the Eastern languages, and the circulation of books, tracts, &c. The prejudice against Christian schools had declined very much at this period, and the Rev. T. Robertson, Secretary to the Committee, remarks on this subject in 1827 : " We require nothing but pecuniary resources, to assemble the

whole youthful population of our Indian villages, where
ever a tree can afford its shade, or a thatched roof give
shelter." A further account of these schools will be given
in the History of the Society for Propagating the Gospel:
the greater part of them, however, were given up in 1839,
in consequence of a resolution of the Society for Propagating the Gospel, withdrawing aid from all schools
which were conducted by heathen teachers, who taught
Christianity in the same way as Grecian mythology is
taught in classical schools in England. In 1842, 3, 4,
the Society supported a school of two hundred heathen
boys in Calcutta, superintended by the Rev. K. Banerji.[i] Several pupils have been sent from this school to
Bishop's College. In 1836, a school for the instruction
of the wretched and debased Portuguese youth of Calcutta was opened by direction of the Bishop in the
Chitpur Road: it flourished for a couple of years under the
superintendance of Mr. C. N. Cooke, but was abandoned
through want of funds.

BOOKS AND TRACTS.—These have proved very useful to
various classes in Bengal, and to none more so than to the
European soldiers: "Formerly soldiers, having no means
of occupying their leisure hours to advantage, buried amid
the jangals of a vast wilderness, yielded themselves up to
dissipation and excess, which, aided by the effect of the
climate, hurried them in the morning of life early victims
to the tomb." In 1818, depôts were formed at Kanhpur,
Mirat, Ghazipur, and Dinapur, under the charge of the

---

[i] This school has of late suffered a diminution in its numbers,
in consequence of a school in its neighbourhood being opened by
Babu Mati Lal Sil, a rich native, the Rothschild of Calcutta, with
a view to empty mission schools; the scheme, however, has failed,
and notwithstanding the denunciations of the Hindus, parents
continue to send their children to institutions where the Scriptures
are taught.

resident chaplains : 800 school books were granted to the chaplain in New South Wales : a supply of books was sent to the little colony in Pitcairn's island, in the South Pacific Ocean. The Lords of the Treasury granted £45 per annum, for the purchase of books, to be distributed, under the direction of the Bishop, among the military in India. In 1821, a circular was addressed by the Society for Promoting Christian Knowledge, to persons at the head of the government offices in Calcutta, requesting them to give information to their Christian writers and clerks of the publications for sale at the depôt of the Society for Promoting Christian Knowledge : the plan succeeded, "a great number of persons thankfully availed themselves of the offer, and purchased a large quantity of books and tracts." In 1824, a depôt was formed in the school-room of St. James's Church, Calcutta, and the Society was "thus enabled to maintain a librarian and native assistant for a less sum than they used to pay their bookseller, and moreover save the per centage upon the books sold." The importance of a depôt may be estimated by the fact, that such a work as Scott's Commentary on the Bible, which now is sold for £5, could not then be procured under £25. Booksellers made rapid fortunes by the enormous profits they gained, while in consequence of their dearness, books of a religious character were almost excluded from sale ; the consequence was, Calcutta was inundated with the trashy novels of the day. Depôts have been formed at various periods in different stations in Bengal : the sale of publications in the Calcutta depôt is steadily on the increase. The Report of 1825 mentions, as an instance of the benefit conferred on soldiers by the Society, the case of a private soldier, who had derived much spiritual consolation from the New Manual of Devotions, while labouring under a fever which he caught when in the field at Arracan, and which terminated in his death. He left £21 8s. 7½d. to the Society. And a gunner, who was also indebted to the same excellent book for most of his religious knowledge and comfort during his last illness, which took place in the General Hospital, left the humbler sum of twelve rupis, as a mark of his gratitude to the Society. "These are proofs that vital religion is inspired amidst scenes of war and sickness through the instrumentality of our Society, whose books can reach the camp and the cot, and convey comfort and instruction in the absence of ministers of religion." Sailors, a class of persons who have, by their drunken and dissolute habits, inflicted deep injury on the cause of Christianity in Bengal, and strengthened the prejudices of the natives against the reception of its sacred truths, also occupied the attention of the Society. "Captains of ships, and other marine officers, are frequently supplied with the Word of God and other sacred books from its depository, at the reduced prices, or gratuitously when it is necessary, for the use of their respective crews." The following are grants made by the Society for Promoting Christian Knowledge in 1833, which show the nature and extent of its operations.

"The Rev. *John Bell*, at *Mhow*, has been supplied with 6 Testaments, 12 Prayer Books, and 246 copies of the Society's publications, as a Lending Library.

"The Rev. Mr. *Prickett* has been supplied with 354 copies of the Society's publications, as a Lending Library for the use of the station of *Bhaugulpore*.

"*Dinapore* has been supplied with 1009 copies of the Society's books and tracts.

"100 Prayer Books and 10 copies of *Sellon's* Abridgment of the Holy Scriptures in *Oordoo* were sent to *Cawnpore*.

"The station of *Dum Dum* has been supplied with 1937 copies of the Society's publications.

"*Cawnpore* received another supply of 10 Bibles, 14 Testaments,

50 Prayer Books, 18 Psalters, and 519 copies of books and tracts.

"*Meerut* has been supplied with 10 Bibles, 15 Testaments, 18 Psalters, and 1370 copies of books and tracts.

"*Barelley* has received 254 copies of the Society's publications.

"The Chaplain of *Fort William*, and the *General Hospital*, have been supplied with 2600 copies of the Society's publications.

"Captain *Lumsden* has been furnished with 1665 copies of the Society's publications, as a Lending Library, and for the use of the station of *Muttra*.

"*Agra* has been supplied with 722 copies of the Society's publications.

"The Minister of the Mariners' Church was furnished with 477 copies of the Society's publications.

"*Cawnpore* again received a supply of 310 copies of the Society's publications.

"The Chaplain of *Fort William*, and the *General Hospital*, were further supplied with 243 copies of the Society's tracts."

In 1821, the number of books sold or given away amounted to 5,885; in 1822, to 5,974; 1823, to 12,286; 1824, to 13,386; 1825, to 7,924; in 1833, to 11,774. The Parent Society has been very liberal; it granted £1000 to Bishop Middleton for Bengal; during the years 1832, 3, 4, 5, 6, it made an annual grant of £500. The Calcutta Depository in 1846 contained a stock of books and tracts amounting in value to £7000.

The Society for Promoting Christian Knowledge established a Circulating Library in Calcutta as early as 1709, the first of the kind in Bengal. Works of a religious and useful nature were, in former days, very scarce, and the Society has, therefore, rendered eminent service by the various depôts of books it formed in different parts of the country, under the superintendence of the chaplains.

Lending Libraries have been formed at the following places by the Society for Promoting Christian Knowledge:—at Chunar in 1823 : "the commanding officer of the European invalids at Chunar, being very desirous of procuring books for the instruction and amusement of the men, during their hours of idleness, which, for want of them, are now given up to dissipation." A short time previously, the East India Company had made a grant of Soldiers' Libraries to the principal European stations. Lending Libraries were formed in 1824, at Kanhpur;[k] in Chittegang and Mirat, 1824; at Agra in 1825; at Gorakhpur and Ghazipur in 1827; at Landour and Bhagalpur in 1829 ; at Muttra, Mhow, and Dum Dum, in 1830; at Maulmain in 1833 ; at Benares in 1834; to the congregation of the Free School Church in Calcutta in 1834.

Sellon's Abridgment of Scripture was translated into Urdu, by Archdeacon Corrie ; and in 1824, 1000 copies of it were printed at the expense of the Society for Promoting Christian Knowledge; the same year 14,000 tracts in the vernacular languages of Bengal had been printed; and 18,000 copies of the Discourses, Miracles, and Parables of Christ, as extracted from the New Testament, were printed in Urdu, Hindu, and Bengali, for the use of schools. The Parables have proved of great use, and very acceptable to the natives, as the greater part of the instruction of Eastern nations is conveyed in an allegorical form. An edition of Watts's Catechism in Bengali, was printed in 1828; in 1839, Bishop Porteus's Evidences were printed in Urdu; in 1841, a translation of "The Brief Explanation of the Catechism," in Bengali, was published.

In 1845, the Society agreed to defray the expenses of a translation of the Book of Common Prayer into the

---

[k] A local committee had been formed there several years previously; they were very active for a time, and held monthly meetings.

Urdu language, for the benefit of the native Christians.
A volume of Sermons has been written in Bengali, and
translations of Bishop Wilson's Tracts on Confirmation
and the Lord's Supper, and the Bishop of Sodor and
Man's (Wilson) Sacra Privata, have been made by
the Rev. K. Banerji, and published at the cost of
the Society; he has been for several years translator to
the Society. A special fund has been formed lately, for
the purpose of defraying the expenses of a series of translations into the Bengali language. In carrying out
Bishop Middleton's plan, it granted £5000, in 1820,
to Bishop's College, as also £6000 for the endowment
of scholarships on the bishop's plan.

The present state of Hindu society calls loudly for
redoubled exertions on the part of the Society for Pro-
moting Christian Knowledge. The works of Paine,
Voltaire, and Gibbon, are extensively read in Bengal.
Superstition is rapidly on the wane: the Bishop of
Calcutta writes on this subject to the Society in 1836:

" India is waiting for the salvation of God. She is moving
on gradually, but surely, towards that measure of illumination,
when the absurd metaphysical abstractions and impure idolatries
of Hinduism must fall, and, together with the intolerant fierce-
ness of Mohammedanism, yield to the benevolence and grace of
Christian truth. It is my earnest prayer that the transition may
be safe, immediate, permanent. The gulf of scepticism yawns
between the prodigious follies, and cruelties, and even unnatural
barbarities of ancient superstitions, and the peaceful doctrine of
the crucified Saviour. To prevent the instructed and inquisitive
natives from falling into that abyss, is one great object I have in
view. They are awakening to Western learning; they ask for
the information which may raise their country to something like
the happiness, and power, and glory of our own. But the spiritual and holy tendencies of Christianity are only slowly opening
upon their understanding. Their own religions, if they may be
called such, they distrust, they neglect. The religion of Englishmen they are eager to learn, so far as the reading of our books
extends."

Useful knowledge and scepticism are spreading. The great desideratum for. India is Christian knowledge. The Society has of late years shown its sense of the importance of a native agency for this object, by its grant of £5000 to the Calcutta Cathedral; but far greater exertions are called for. American booksellers have sent hundreds of copies of Paine's Age of Reason to Calcutta; and the Indian market has been inundated with obscene French prints.

We conclude this short sketch of the operations of the Society for Promoting Christian Knowledge, with a specimen of the exertions of "Young Bengal." In 1845, a publication was issued from the Calcutta press, called " General Reflections on Christianity, containing a brief and philosophical Exposition of the folly of believing in the Divine Origin of Christianity, and relying on it for human salvation, by Collycoomer Doss, President of the Calcutta Phrenological Society." The author professes to account for the miracles of Christ by the laws of phrenology.

The Society for Promoting Christian Knowledge in Bengal during the last century had to contend with apathy and idolatry: but a different class of opponents now present themselves. Education without religion is spreading rapidly. Some, however, are of opinion that the renunciation of idolatry, and consequent scepticism, is a transition state favourable for Christianity. "There might be a moral as well as natural twilight between darkness and the broad and open daylight: there might be the reflected rays before the Sun of Righteousness bursts forth in splendour above the horizon." Six thousand natives are studying English in Calcutta; and many of them have attained such proficiency in English science and literature, that the government of Bengal have recommended to the Court of Directors the establishment of an University in Calcutta. A class called "Young Bengal" has arisen, repudiating the customs and practices of their fore-fathers. A couple of *English* periodicals are edited by natives in Calcutta. The Medical College of Calcutta furnishes natives with a medical education equal to that given in England.

Respecting the prospects of usefulness opening out to the Society, the Rev. K. M. Banerji makes the following remarks in a letter to Archdeacon Dealtry :—

"With reference to what may yet be done, the field is vast and wide. The demands of Christians and inquirers are very extensive; and where are they to look for supplies, if not to your Committee and the Syndicate of Bishop's College? We need an authorised version of the Holy Scriptures. The existing translations are unsatisfactory, varied, and fluctuating. There is no book in Bengali which the native Christian can call *his Bible* with the same satisfaction with which an Englishman is privileged to look upon his. The disadvantages, proceeding from this want, are so evident, that they need not be repeated.

"We require also a body of apologetic and dogmatic divinity—that the doubts of inquirers and the cravings of catechumens may be satisfied, and the Christian's growth in grace assisted by instructive and edifying books.

"Works on Church history and Ecclesiastical antiquities are likewise wanted. It is of the last importance that the Christian should know the annals of his Church, the way in which the *smallest grain* of mustard-seed to which our Saviour likened the kingdom of heaven, grew up into a large and wide-spreading tree; the platform whereon the gospel triumphed against heathenism, heresy, and schism; the faith and patience of its planters and their successors; the constancy and cheerfulness with which martyrs preferred death to a denial of Christ. The knowledge of all these, must tend to build up our infant churches in faith, hope, and charity.

"Hinduism and Mohammedanism, too, must be refuted. The groundless claims of the impostor, and the unauthorised monstro sities of Hinduism, esoteric and exoteric, must be exposed. But who, I again ask, can do all this, if not your Committee, assisted

by the Syndicate of Bishop's College, in dependence upon God
—especially when the consummation of the Lord Bishop's plans
concerning the New Cathedral takes place.

"The resources requisite for the supplies of these demands
must be large in every respect—and in the ordinary dispensa-
tions of Providence, great things require length of time. But I
sincerely hope that no Christian will therefore be wanting in his
own duties to his Church in this respect. If those to whom
wealth has been vouchsafed enrich your hands, if scholars devote
their talents, and if every one invokes God's blessing upon your
exertions, then we may expect the gradual supply of all that is
needed."

*The preceding account of the operations in the Bengal Presidency
of the Society for Promoting Christian Knowledge, forms the first
part of a volume which has been just published in London, entitled,
" History of the Church of England Missions in North India,
with a comprehensive view of educational effort in Bengal. By the
Rev. J. Long, Missionary from Calcutta."*

www.ingramcontent.com/pod-product-compliance
Lightning Source LLC
Chambersburg PA
CBHW081307040426
42452CB00014B/2679